Phonics Tales!

OO

Goo, Goo!

by Teddy Slater
illustrated by Cary Pillo

D0564591

SCHOLASTIC INC.

New York • Toronto • London • Auckland • Sydney
Mexico City • New Dehli • Hong Kong • Buenos Aires

Designed by Maria Lilja
ISBN-13: 978-0-439-88462-4 • ISBN-10: 0-439-88462-4
Copyright © 2006 by Scholastic Inc.
All rights reserved. Printed in the U.S.A.

First printing, November 2006

12 11 10 9 8 7 6 5 4 3 2 1   6 7 8 9 10 11/0

Everyone thinks my brother is **too** cute for words. "Kitchy, kitchy, **coo**!" they say. "**Ooh**, he is so sweet!" they **croon**.

But all my brother says is, "**Goo, goo!**" He is **too** little to talk. He just opens up his **googly** eyes. Then he smiles his **goofy** grin and **drools**.

Speech bubbles in illustration: "Hoo", "Moo!"

My brother's **room** is like a **zoo**. He has a **moose**, a **goose**, a **raccoon**, a **poodle**, a **baboon**, and a big **kangaroo**.

He has an owl that says, "**Hoot**!" and a cow that says, "**Moo**!" Everyone gives him stuffed animals.

But does my brother say thanks? Nope.
He just says, "**Goo, goo!**" That is all he can say:
"**Goo, goo! Goo, goo!**"

My brother likes my toys, **too**. I have a car that
goes **VROOM** and a plane that goes **ZOOM**.
I have a drum that goes **BOOM! BOOM! BOOM!**
And I have a **choo**-choo train with
a red **caboose**.

My brother has just one **tooth**, so he only eats
gooey foods. "**Goo, goo!**" he says when you
give him a **noodle**. He can't even use a **spoon**!

After lunch, his eyes get **droopy**. Sometimes he even **snoozes** all **afternoon**.

Phonics Fact

Sometimes *oo* is pronounced differently than in the words **too**, **ooh**, and **goo, goo**. It can also make the sound found in *good*, *wood*, and *took*. Can you find a word on page 11 with the same *oo* sound as in *good*?

(Answer: **books**)

But as **soon** as I come home from **school**, he wakes up. Then he gives me that good old grin and we play and play!

10

At night, in the **moonlight**, I help Mom put on his **booties**. She reads him fun books like *Winnie the Pooh.* After that, I **toot** my **kazoo** and sing "Yankee **Doodle** Dandy."

If he is not in the **mood** to sleep, my brother cries, "**Boo, hoo**! **Boo, hoo**!" My parents try **oodles** of things to make him stop. But I'm the only one who can.

I **scoot** over to his crib, **scoop** him up, and give him a big **smooch**. And just like that, he goes from "**Boo, hoo**!" to "**Goo, goo**!"

That's the **cool** thing about the kid. I love him and he loves me, **too**! If I could pick any brother, I would always **choose** him!